Dale Murphy
Baseball's Gentle Giant

Patricia Stone Martin

illustrated by Bernard Doctor

Rourke Enterprises ⚊ Vero Beach, Florida

Manufactured in the United States of America

Library of Congress Cataloging-in-Publication Data

Martin, Patricia Stone.
   Dale Murphy – baseball's gentle giant.

   (Reaching your goal biographies)
   Summary: Traces the life of the popular Atlanta Braves
centerfielder who captured his third straight Golden
Glove award in 1984. Includes information on setting
goals.
   1. Murphy, Dale, 1956-   – Juvenile literature.
2. Baseball players – United States – Biography –
Juvenile literature. [1. Murphy, Dale, 1956-
2. Baseball players] I. Title. II. Series:
Martin, Patricia Stone. Reaching your goal biographies.
GV865.M79M37 1987 796.357'092'4 [B] [92] 87-13012
ISBN 0-86592-167-9

It was ten-year-old Dale's turn at bat. He had just joined Little League. He loved baseball. His dad played catch with him. Popo, his grandfather, encouraged him to play. Dale's great-grandfather had even played semi-pro baseball. But would all of that help him now?

Dale took his place at home plate. He looked carefully at the pitcher. It was Dale's first time up against John Dunn. John had thrown 17 no-hitters! Dale held on to his bat. He swung a few times to get the feel of it. Suddenly the ball was there. Whack! Dale had made a hit! Everyone cheered. Dale's parents were proud of him. Popo was proud of him.

Today Dale Murphy plays for the Atlanta Braves. He is one of the team's most popular and best players.

Dale Murphy was born on March 12, 1956, in Portland, Oregon. He was the second child in the family. His older sister was named Susan.

Dale grew up playing all kinds of sports. He says, "The important thing is to have fun playing." Dale does not think kids should take sports too seriously. They should play because they enjoy it.

Dale played basketball and football in high school. His best sport was baseball. He was hitting over .400 by his senior year. He was named All-City and All-State.

Dale graduated from high school in 1974. Scouts from the major league ball clubs had seen him play. The Atlanta Braves hired him. He was their first choice. They sent him to a rookie league team in Kingsport, Tennessee, to get experience. Rookies are first-year players. The Braves said Dale would be a great catcher.

The next year, Dale was moved up to a Class A team. His batting average went down. But that year an important change happened in Dale's life. Dale started going to church. He learned about Jesus Christ. From then on his belief in God was very important to him.

In 1976, Dale won a place on the Class AA team. He played so well he moved up to a Class AAA team that same year. Soon Dale was ready to leave the minor leagues and play for the Braves. He went to Atlanta to be a catcher.

But suddenly Dale had trouble throwing the ball. The other team stole bases, and Dale could not stop them. In 1977 Dale was sent back to the minor leagues. He needed time to work on his throw.

The next year Dale was back playing for Atlanta again. He started the season as a catcher. Then he was moved to first base. He drove in 79 runs and hit 23 home runs that year. During the off-season, Dale went to college. There he met Nancy Thomas.

Dale began the 1979 season playing well. Then he hurt his knee. He only hit 21 home runs that year. In October Dale and Nancy were married.

In 1980 Dale played left field. Then he was moved to center field. He had finally found his best position. At 6 feet, 5 inches tall, Dale was one of baseball's tallest center fielders. He hit 33 home runs that year. He was named to the National League All-Star team. That summer he and Nancy had their first baby. It was a boy, and they named him Chad.

In 1981, the baseball teams went on strike. No games were played until the strike was settled. Both players and fans were unhappy: But something good also happened that year. The Murphys had another baby boy. They named him Travis.

The Atlanta Braves had a great year in 1982. They won their first 13 games! They also won the National League title. Dale won the Gold Glove Award as the best defensive center fielder. The fans voted him to the National League All-Star team. He was chosen as the National League's Most Valuable Player. In December, Dale and Nancy had Shawn, their third son.

The next year Dale won the Gold Glove Award again. And again he was chosen for the All-Star team. He won the Most Valuable Player Award for the second year in a row!

But as the 1984 season began, Dale was not playing his best game. One day he was so upset that he kicked the water cooler in the dugout. He did not usually act this way. He knew he had to change. He made himself relax. He began to play better than ever. He hit 36 home runs that year and won his third Gold Glove Award. He was also chosen for the All-Star team again.

In December 1985 Nancy and Dale had their fourth son, named Tyson. Dale jokes that he is growing his own baseball team.

His family and God come first in Dale's life. Baseball comes second. Dale spends as much time with his family as he can. He likes to play ball with his sons. To him, teamwork is very important. "I don't want people to ever think I am better than anyone else," Dale has said. He sees himself as just one of the team.

Dale was on the All-Star team in both 1985 and 1986. Many people think he will be named into baseball's Hall of Fame someday. Dale does not drink, use drugs, smoke, or chew tobacco. He works hard to do his best, and everyone likes him.

Even if Dale never played in another baseball game, he has already reached many of his goals. He is a good husband, a good father, a good church worker, a good ball player, and a good person.

Reaching Your Goal

What are your goals? Here are some steps to help you reach them.

1. **Decide on your goal.**
   It may be a short-term goal like one of these:
   learning to ride a bike
   getting a good grade on a test
   keeping your room clean
   It may be a long-term goal like one of these:
   learning to read
   learning to play the piano
   becoming a lawyer

2. **Decide if your goal is something you really can do.**
   Do you have the talent you need?
   How can you find out? By trying!
   Will you need special equipment?
   Perhaps you need a piano or ice skates.
   How can you get what you need?
   Ask your teacher or your parents.

3. Decide on the first thing you must do.

Perhaps this will be to take lessons.

4. Decide on the second thing you must do.

Perhaps this will be to practice every day.

5. Start right away.

Stick to your plan until you reach your goal.

6. Keep telling yourself, "I can do it!"

Good luck! Maybe you will become a great baseball player like Dale Murphy!

Reaching Your Goal Books

Beverly Cleary
She Makes Reading Fun

Bill Cosby Superstar

Jesse Jackson A Rainbow Leader

Ted Kennedy, Jr.
A Lifetime of Challenges

Christa McAuliffe
Reaching for the Stars

Dale Murphy
Baseball's Gentle Giant

Dr. Seuss We Love You

Samantha Smith Young Ambassador

Rourke Enterprises, Inc.
P.O. Box 3328
Vero Beach, FL 32964